AMAZING PLANET
SCRATCH AWAY
ACTIVITY BOOK

make
believe
ideas

GUESS WHERE!

Draw a <u>line</u> to join each fact
with the place you think it matches.

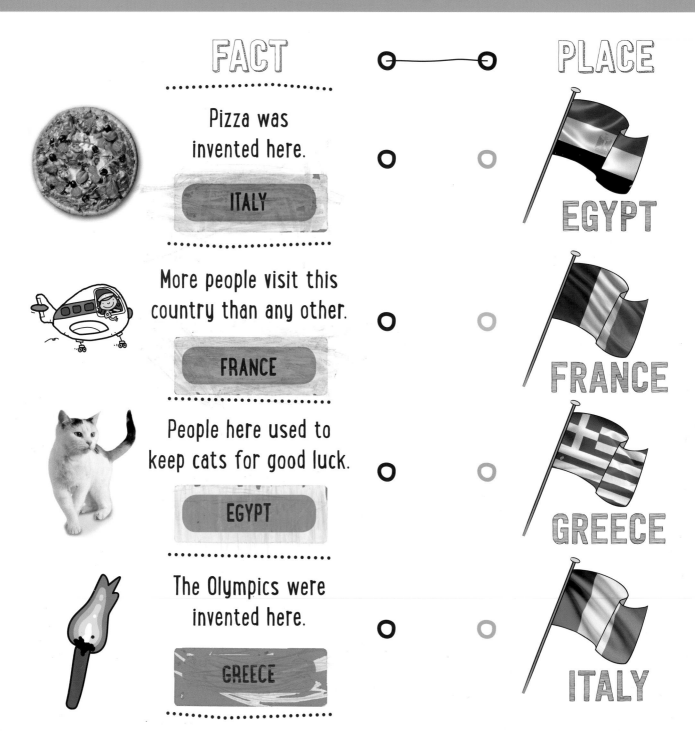

FACT   PLACE

Pizza was
invented here.

ITALY

EGYPT

More people visit this
country than any other.

FRANCE

FRANCE

People here used to
keep cats for good luck.

EGYPT

GREECE

The Olympics were
invented here.

GREECE

ITALY

>> Scratch off the panels to see if you were right! <<

Guess what made the loudest sound ever recorded!

Scratch off the clues one by one. Cross out the pictures that don't match each description, then scratch off the panel when you think you know the answer.

1 It's not a vehicle. <<

2 It's not a living thing. <<

3 It isn't manmade. <<

4 It has magma inside! <<

VOLCANIC ERUPTION

COMET FALLING

LION ROARING

THUNDER AND LIGHTNING

EARTHQUAKE

ROCKET BLASTOFF!

BOMB

MUSIC CONCERT

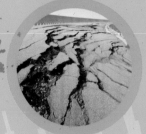

BLUE WHALE

FIRE TRUCK

I KNOW THE ANSWER!

A volcano in Indonesia erupted with so much power that the sound could be heard in Australia!

CARROTS

FIREWORKS

GOING GLOBAL!

Look at the map and guess where each of the seven continents is.

North America ★ Europe ★ Asia ★ South America

Africa ★ Australia ★ Antarctica

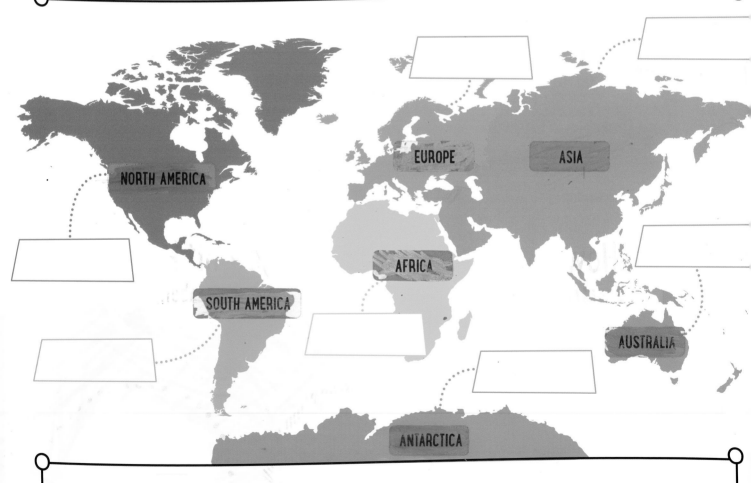

Once you have made your guesses, scratch off the panels to see if you were right!

Mummy maze

Scratch off the panels as you move through the maze.
Try not to hit too many mummies!

Start

Finish

How many mummies did you hit?
Scratch off the circle underneath the correct number.

0–3   4–5   6–7

Quick-fire quiz!

Where are you most likely to find sand?

- [ ] IN ICELAND
- [ ] IN SCOTLAND
- [x] IN EGYPT

CLUE

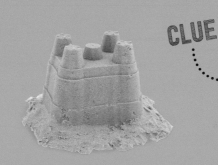

Which country is the hottest?

- [x] AUSTRALIA
- [ ] NORWAY
- [ ] CANADA

Which country is famous for spaghetti?

- [x] ITALY
- [ ] FRANCE
- [ ] USA

Where won't you find penguins?

- [x] SOUTH AFRICA
- [x] ALASKA
- [x] AUSTRALIA

Where would you find the Amazon river?

 BRAZIL

 ENGLAND

 EGYPT

Where are you most likely to find snow?

 IN THE DESERT

 IN THE SEA

 AT THE NORTH POLE

Where would you be most likely to find fossils?

 IN SNOW

 IN SAND

 IN ROCKS

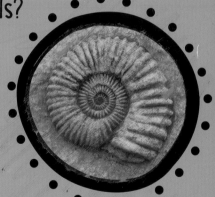

What is the tallest mountain in the world?

 MOUNT EVEREST

 TABLE MOUNTAIN

 MOUNT KILIMANJARO

RIDDLE ME THIS!

Treasure is buried under one of the objects on the map. Solve the riddle, then scratch off the panel below the correct object to find the treasure!

I have no wings, so I move on silk strings.

N

GUESS AGAIN

TREASURE!

Solve these riddles about objects on the map.
Once you know the answer, scratch off the panel to see if you got it right!

Stomp on my head, and I don't hurt.
You can use me to move dirt.

Up and down I always go,
but I never move or grow.

GO WITH THE FLOW!

Answer each question to choose your path.
Scratch off the arrow you follow. If it is green, you got the question right. If it is red, you got the question wrong.

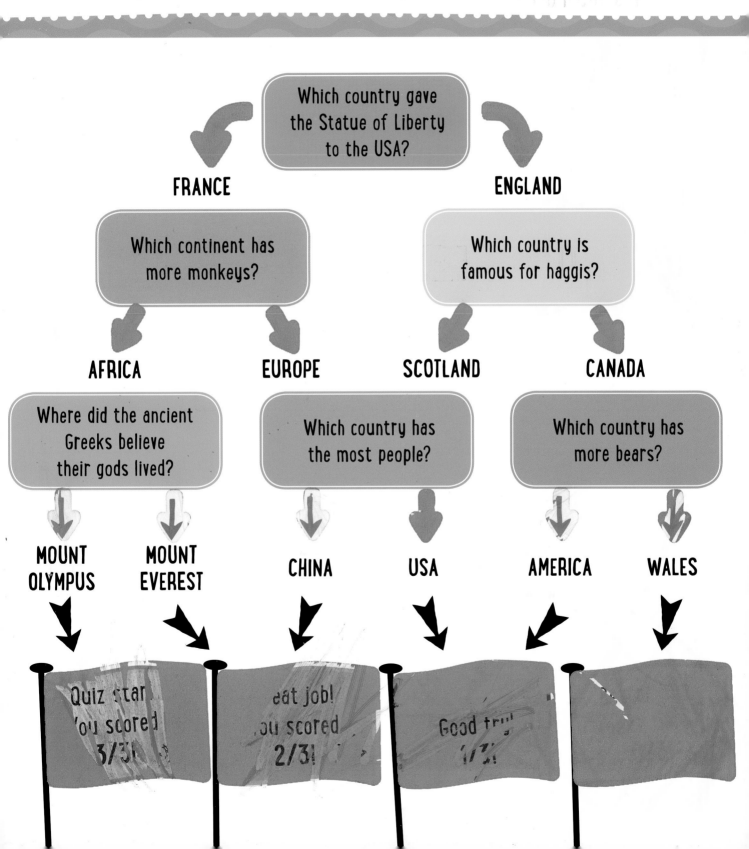

GUESS WHERE!

Draw a <u>line</u> to join each fact with the place you think it matches.

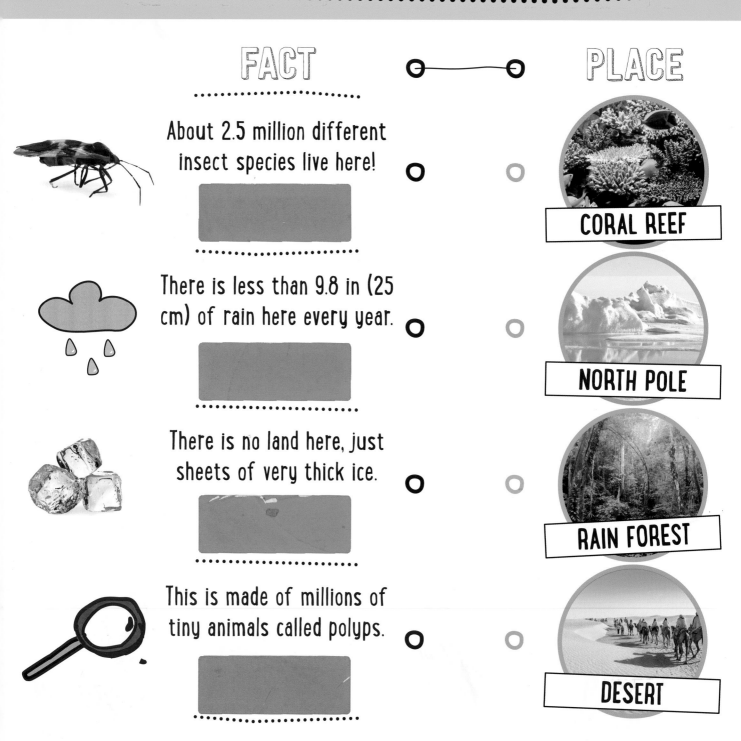

FACT — PLACE

About 2.5 million different insect species live here!

There is less than 9.8 in (25 cm) of rain here every year.

There is no land here, just sheets of very thick ice.

This is made of millions of tiny animals called polyps.

CORAL REEF

NORTH POLE

RAIN FOREST

DESERT

>> Scratch off the panels to see if you were right! <<

Guess what the biggest living thing in the world is!

Scratch off the clues one by one. Cross out the pictures that don't match each description, then scratch off the circle when you think you know the answer.

1 <<   **3** <<

2 <<   **4** <<

SEAWEED

CRAB

BLUE WHALE

MUSHROOM

ELEPHANT

GIRAFFE

I KNOW THE ANSWER!

The largest living thing in the world is a **mushroom!** It grows under a forest in Oregon, USA, and covers 2,200 acres of land.

TURNIP

SNAIL

CROCODILE

FLOWERS

TREE

PIG

AROUND THE WORLD

Guess where these famous buildings are!

Write your guesses under the pictures, then scratch off the panels to find out if you were right. Can you guess the city for bonus fun?

. . . .

. . . .

. . . .

. . . .

. . . .

. . . .

Coral craze!

Scratch off the panels as you move through the maze.
Try not to hit too many corals.

Start
v

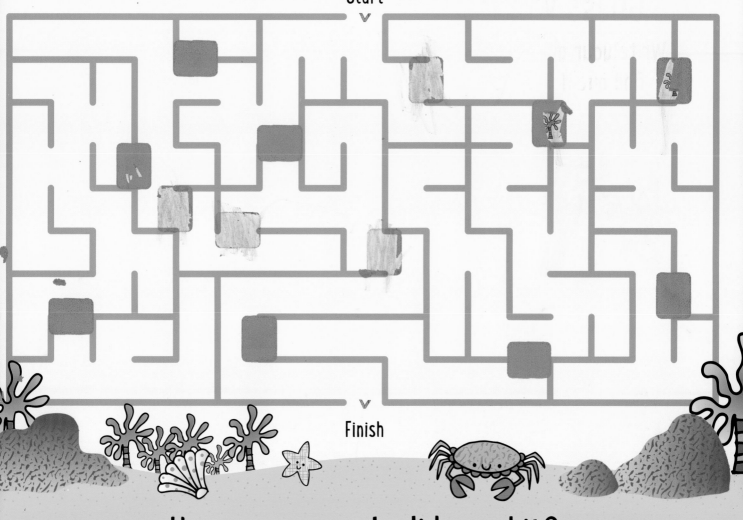

v
Finish

How many corals did you hit?

Scratch off the circle underneath the correct number.

0-3   4-5   6-7

  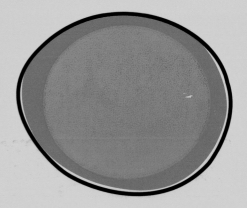

Quick-fire quiz!

Where would you be most likely to find a glacier?

- ☐ EGYPT
- ☐ ICELAND
- ☐ ITALY

CLUE

Which one is a tropical rain forest?

- ☐ BLACK FOREST, GERMANY
- ☐ THE AMAZON, BRAZIL
- ☐ CROOKED FOREST, POLAND

Where in the world can it be light all day long?

- ☐ ANTARCTICA
- ☐ THE SAHARA
- ☐ MADAGASCAR

What is the capital of Greece?

- ☐ ROME
- ☐ POMPEII
- ☐ ATHENS

Which country is famous for noodles?

☐ **CHINA**

☐ **SWITZERLAND**

☐ **WALES**

Where is the Taj Mahal?

☐ **SAUDI ARABIA**

☒ **INDIA**

☐ **DUBAI**

Where is the Loch Ness Monster supposed to live?

☑ **SCOTLAND**

☒ **WALES**

☒ **IRELAND**

What is the world's tallest waterfall?

☐ **NIAGARA FALLS**

☐ **YOSEMITE FALLS**

☐ **ANGEL FALLS**

RIDDLE ME THIS!

Treasure is buried under one of the objects on the map. Solve the riddle, then scratch off the panel below the correct object to find the treasure!

I'm made of snow, but I'll keep you warm.

N

TREASURE!

Solve these riddles about objects on the map.
Once you know the answer, scratch off the panel to see if you got it right!

Building me can be such fun,
but I melt under the Sun.

Don't use me to close your letter;
swimming is what I do better.

GO WITH THE FLOW!

Answer each question to choose your path.
Scratch off the arrow you follow. If it is green, you got the question right. If it is red, you got the question wrong.

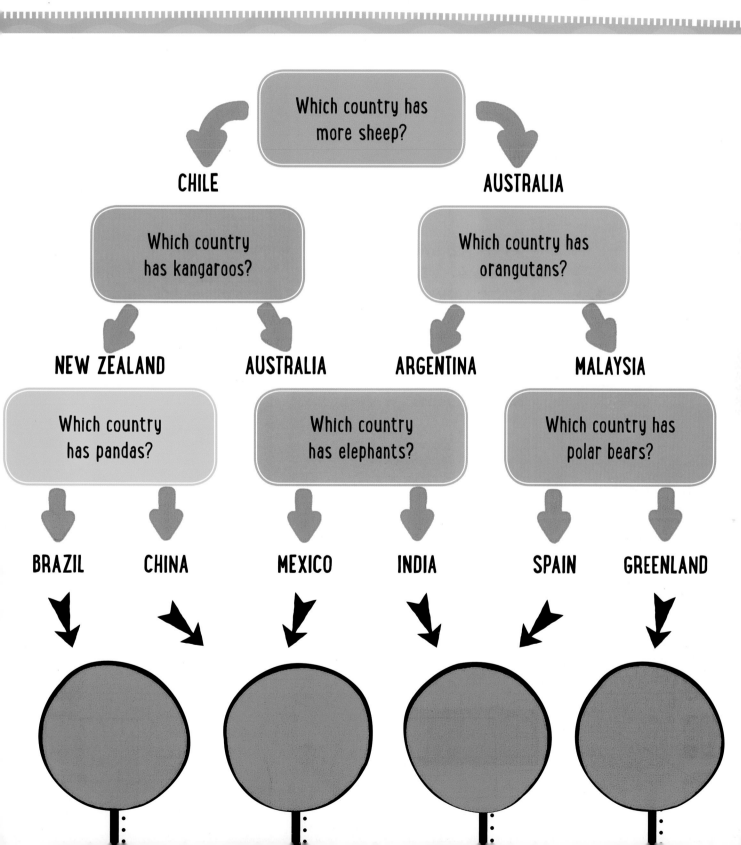

GUESS WHERE!

★ ★ ★ ★ ★ ★ ★ ★ ★ ★ ★ ★

Draw a <u>line</u> to join each fact with the picture you think it matches.

★ ★ ★ ★ ★ ★ ★ ★ ★

FACT ○—○ **PLACE**

This is the only planet in the solar system not to be named after an ancient god! ○ ○

THE SUN

This shines because it reflects light from the Sun. ○ ○

EARTH

This can also be called the Red Planet. ○ ○

MARS

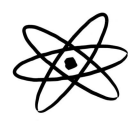

All of the planets orbit around this. ○ ○

THE MOON

>> Scratch off the panels to see if you were right! <<

Guess what the oldest living thing on earth is!

Scratch off the clues one by one. Cross out the pictures that don't match each description, then scratch off the panel when you think you know the answer.

1 <<   **3** <<

2 <<   **4** <<

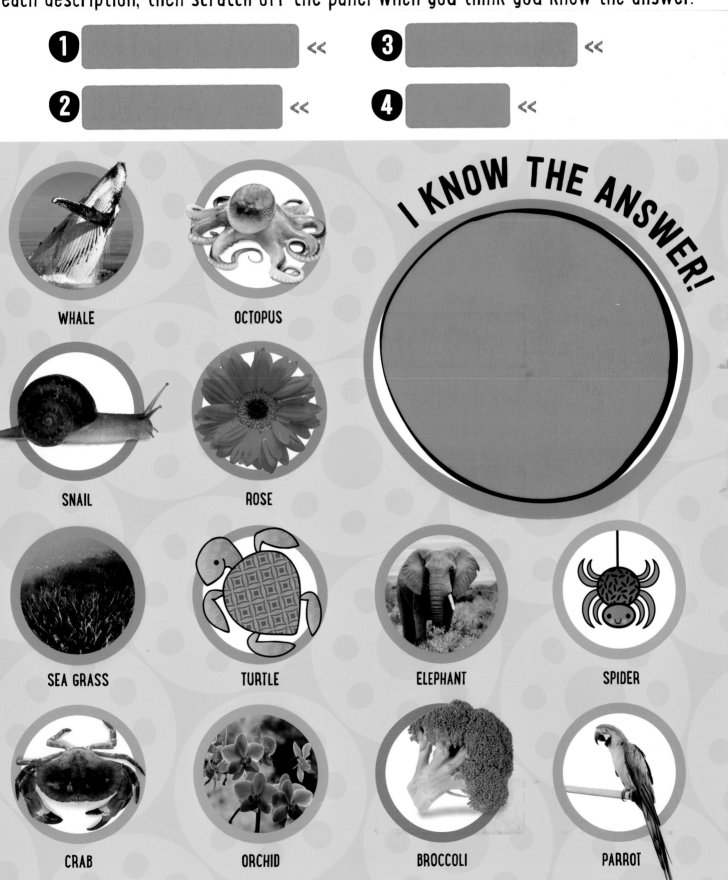

WHALE   OCTOPUS

I KNOW THE ANSWER!

SNAIL   ROSE

SEA GRASS   TURTLE   ELEPHANT   SPIDER

CRAB   ORCHID   BROCCOLI   PARROT

SCRATCH FACTS

Guess the names of these landmarks!

Write your guesses under the pictures, then scratch off the panels to find out if you were right. Can you guess the country for bonus fun?

To infinity!

Scratch off the panels as you move through the maze.
Try not to hit too many satellites.

Start
∨

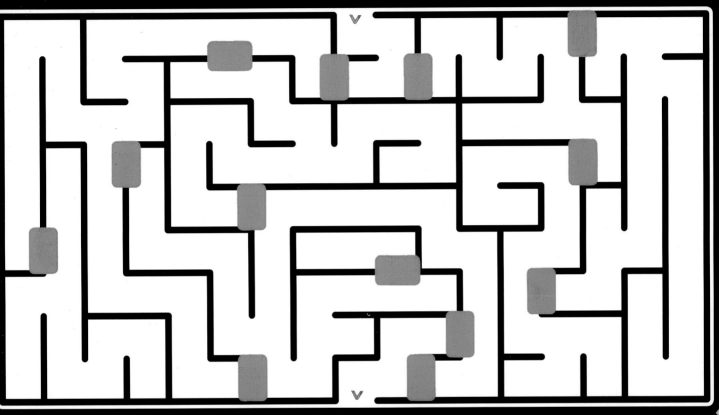

∨
Finish

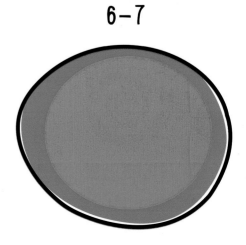

How many satellites did you hit?
Scratch off the circle underneath the correct number.

0 – 3   4 – 5   6 – 7

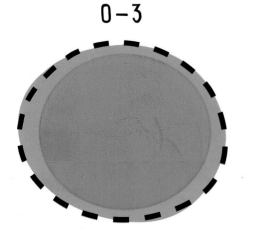
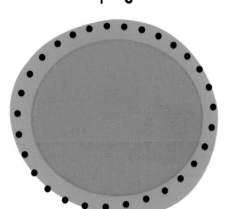

Quick-fire quiz!

Which country is famous for sausages?

 ✓ GERMANY

 PORTUGAL

USA

 CLUE

What is the biggest country in the world?

 ✗ INDIA

 SOUTH AFRICA

 ✓ RUSSIA

Where is Mount Everest?

 ✓ NEPAL

 SWITZERLAND

 FRANCE

 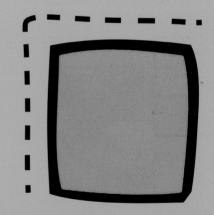

The equator runs around the . . . of the earth.

 TOP

 ✓ MIDDLE

 BOTTOM

 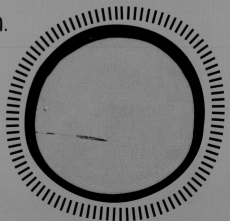

Which country is famous for apple pie?

- [ ] IRELAND
- [x] USA
- [ ] EGYPT

Which country has the most volcanoes?

- [ ] AUSTRALIA
- [ ] NIGERIA
- [x] INDONESIA

Where will you find the largest number of lakes in the world?

- [x] CANADA
- [ ] AUSTRALIA
- [ ] RUSSIA

Where are you more likely to find rhinos?

- [ ] EUROPE
- [x] AFRICA
- [ ] NORTH AMERICA

RIDDLE ME THIS!

Treasure is buried under one of the objects on the map. Solve the riddle, then scratch off the panel below the correct object to find the treasure!

All I am is holes and string, but I can hold almost anything!

TREASURE!

Solve these riddles about objects on the map.
Once you know the answer, scratch off the panel to see if you got it right!

Look on the back of a snail or crab. I can be pretty; I can be drab.

Fit for a king, but quite small. A wave could break down my wall.

GO WITH THE FLOW!

Answer each question to choose your path.
Scratch off the arrow you follow. If it is green, you got the question right. If it is red, you got the question wrong.

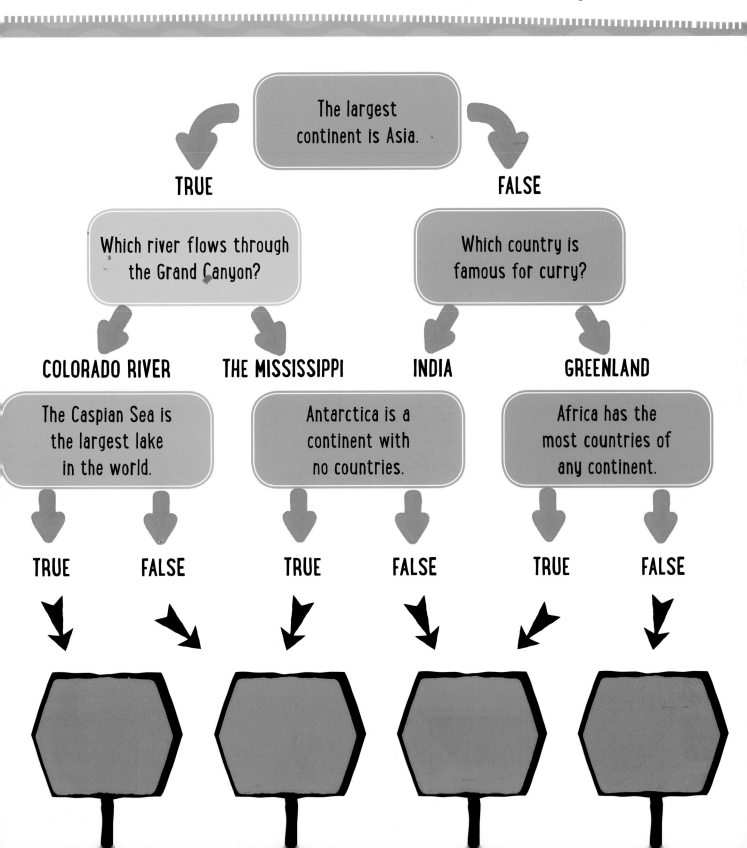

The largest continent is Asia.

TRUE

FALSE

Which river flows through the Grand Canyon?

Which country is famous for curry?

COLORADO RIVER

THE MISSISSIPPI

INDIA

GREENLAND

The Caspian Sea is the largest lake in the world.

Antarctica is a continent with no countries.

Africa has the most countries of any continent.

TRUE

FALSE

TRUE

FALSE

TRUE

FALSE

GUESS WHERE!

Draw a <u>line</u> to join each fact
with the place you think it matches.

FACT

PLACE

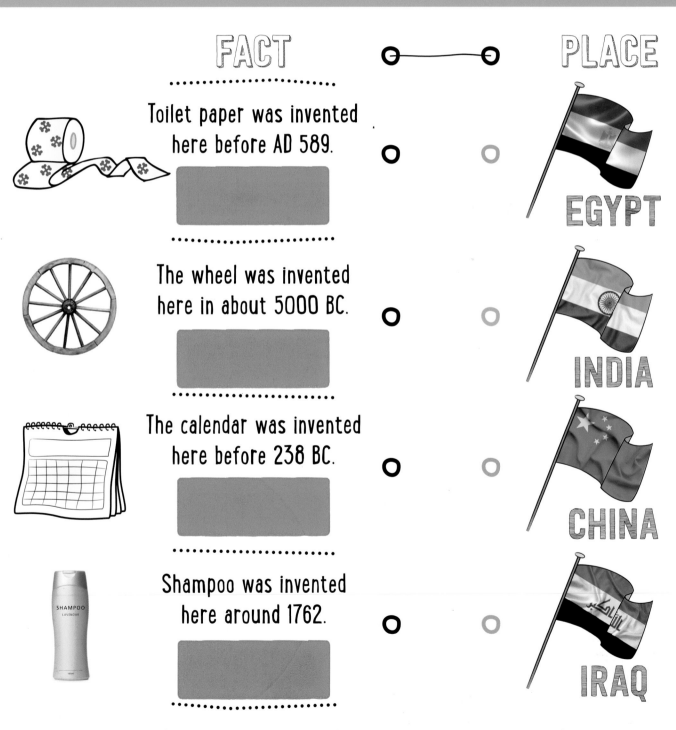

Toilet paper was invented here before AD 589.

The wheel was invented here in about 5000 BC.

The calendar was invented here before 238 BC.

Shampoo was invented here around 1762.

EGYPT

INDIA

CHINA

IRAQ

>> Scratch off the panels to see if you were right! <<

Guess which animal the ancient Egyptians used as a symbol for great power.

1 ▢ ≪   **3** ▢ ≪

2 ▢ ≪   **4** ▢ ≪

RABBIT

PENGUINS

FISH

BULL

HORSE

ELEPHANT

DUNG BEETLE

DONKEY

FROG

CAMEL

I KNOW THE ANSWER!

HIPPO

BUTTERFLY

 # SCRATCH FACTS

Three-quarters of the world is covered in water.
Can you guess where these oceans are?

Pacific Ocean ★ Atlantic Ocean ★ Indian Ocean

Southern Ocean ★ Arctic Ocean

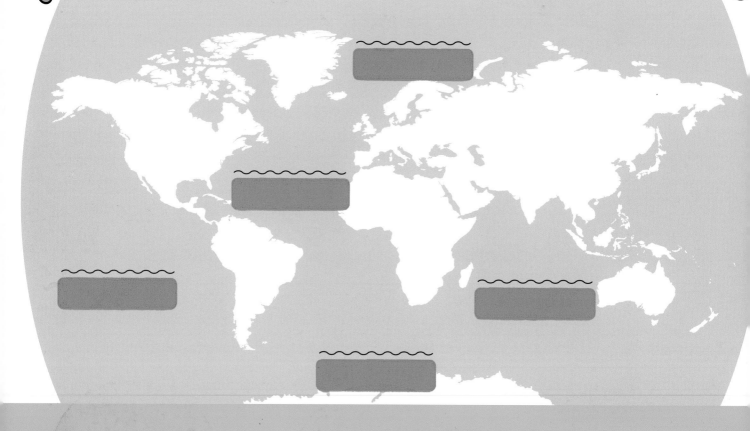

> > > > > > > Once you have made your guesses, scratch
off the panels to see if you were right! < < < < < <

It's all Greek to me!

Scratch off the panels as you move through the maze.
Try not to hit too many pillars.

Start >

Finish

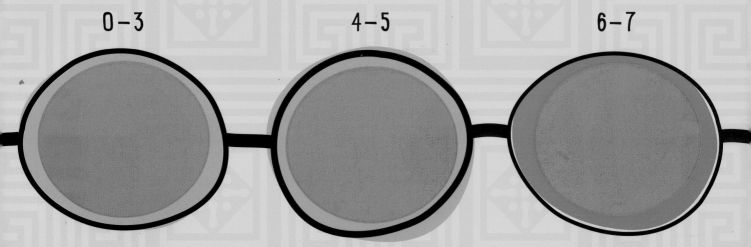

How many pillars did you hit?
Scratch off the circle underneath the correct number.

0–3   4–5   6–7

Quick-fire quiz!

About how much of the Earth is covered in water?

- ONE-QUARTER
- ONE-HALF
- THREE-QUARTERS

CLUE

Which is the biggest ocean in the world?

- PACIFIC
- ATLANTIC
- ARCTIC

About how much of the Earth is covered in tropical rain forest?

- ONE-HALF
- ONE-SIXTEENTH
- THREE-QUARTERS

Which continent is closest to Antarctica?

- SOUTH AMERICA
- AUSTRALIA
- AFRICA

S

About how much of the earth is covered in ice?

1%

10%

50%

Which country is closest to the North Pole?

SAUDI ARABIA

INDIA

GREENLAND

N

Finish the name of this famous landmark: The Great Wall of . . .

CHINA

RUSSIA

PAKISTAN

A book containing lots of maps is called . . .

A COMPASS

AN ATLAS

A MAPLASS

MAP

RIDDLE ME THIS!

Treasure is buried under one of the objects on the map. Solve the riddle, then scratch off the panel below the correct object to find the treasure!

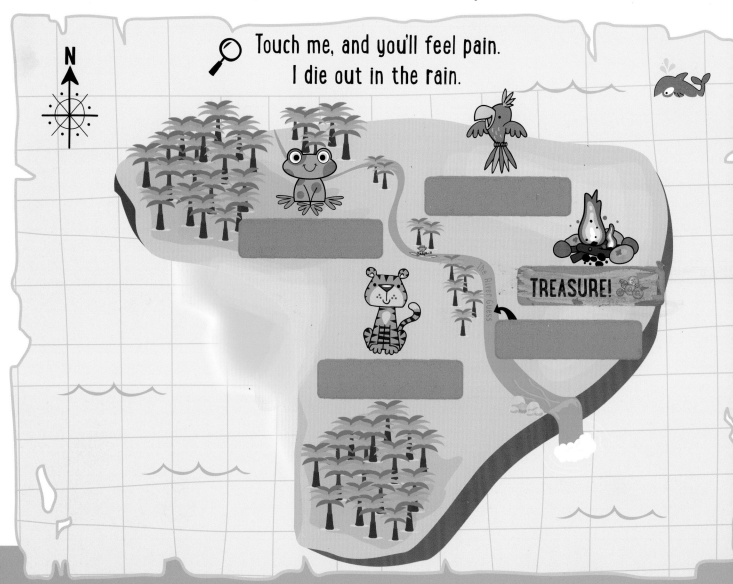

Touch me, and you'll feel pain.
I die out in the rain.

TREASURE!

The River Guess

Solve these riddles about objects on the map.
Once you know the answer, scratch off the panel to see if you got it right!

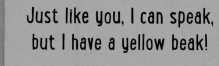

I don't have legs, but I run all day.
I have a mouth, but no words to say.

Just like you, I can speak,
but I have a yellow beak!

GO WITH THE FLOW!

Answer each question to choose your path.
Scratch off the arrow you follow. If it is green, you got the
question right. If it is red, you got the question wrong.

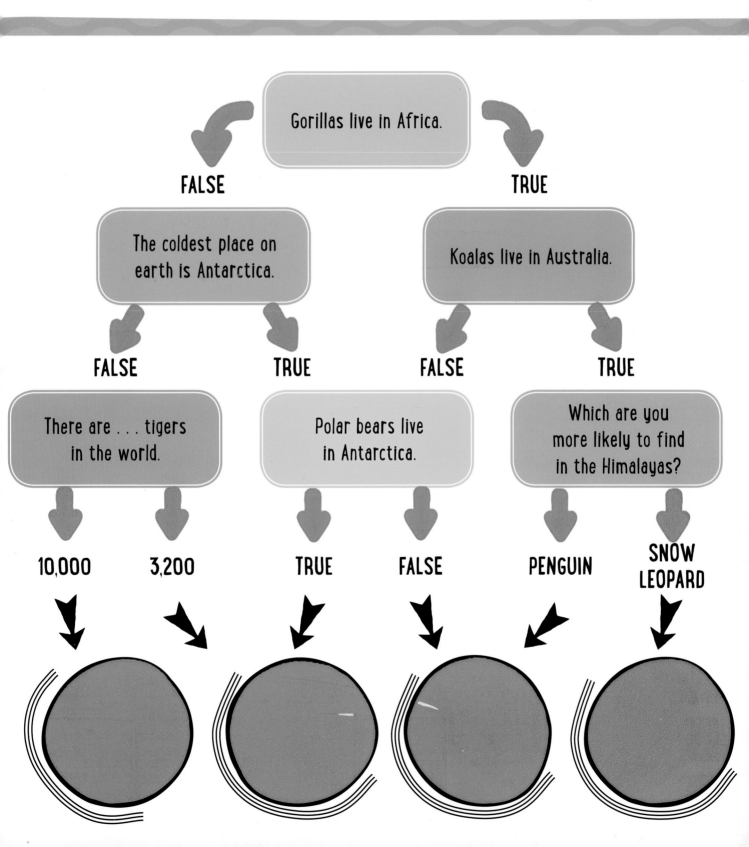

Gorillas live in Africa.

FALSE

TRUE

The coldest place on
earth is Antarctica.

Koalas live in Australia.

FALSE

TRUE

FALSE

TRUE

There are . . . tigers
in the world.

Polar bears live
in Antarctica.

Which are you
more likely to find
in the Himalayas?

10,000

3,200

TRUE

FALSE

PENGUIN

SNOW
LEOPARD

GUESS WHERE! ?

Draw a <u>line</u> to join each outfit
with the place you think it comes from.

FACT ○———○ PLACE

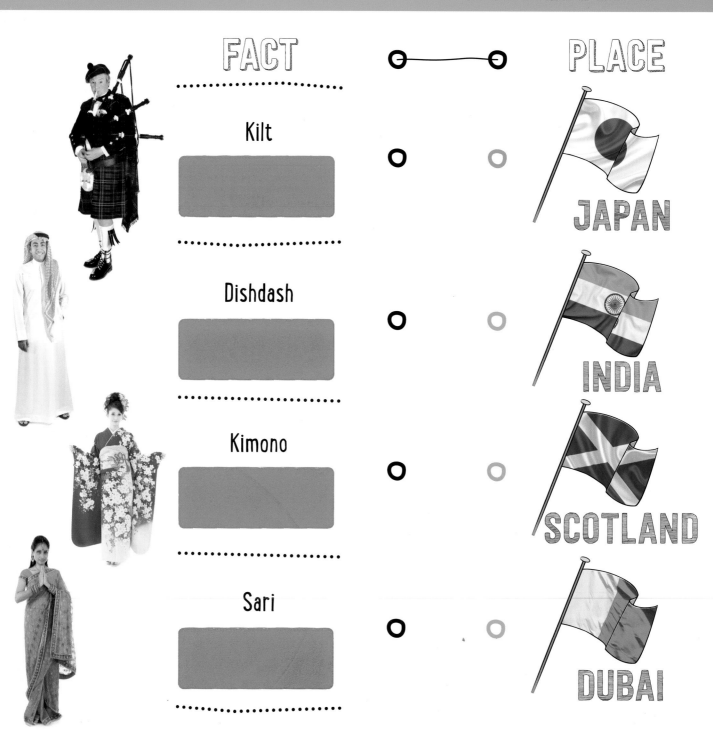

Kilt

Dishdash

Kimono

Sari

JAPAN

INDIA

SCOTLAND

DUBAI

>> Scratch off the panels to see if you were right! <<

Guess what builds the biggest nests in the world!

Scratch off the clues one by one. Cross out the pictures that don't match each description, then scratch off the panel when you think you know the answer.

1 [ ] «

2 [ ] «

3 [ ] «

4 [ ] «

BALD EAGLE

HORSE

HEN

SNAKE

ANT

RACCOON

GORILLA

FROG

PARROT

TOUCAN

I KNOW THE ANSWER!

WASP

PENGUIN

CLEVER COMPASS

Use the compass to finish the directions for the girl. Then scratch off the panels to see if you were right.

1 To get to the ship, she should travel ....

2 To get to the cave, she should travel ....

3 To get to the tractor, she should travel ....

4 To get to the cow, she should travel ....

5 To get to the pond, she should travel ....

Dinosaur escape

Scratch off the panels as you move through the maze.
Try not to hit too many dinos.

Start

Finish

How many dinos did you hit?
Scratch off the circle underneath the correct number.

0 - 3   4 - 5   6 - 7

Quick-fire quiz!

Where are you more likely to find a camel?

- [ ] CANADA
- [ ] INDONESIA
- [✓] EGYPT

Which country uses dragons as a symbol for luck?

- [✓] CHINA
- [ ] USA
- [ ] CHILE

Russia is a . . .

- [ ] CONTINENT
- [✓] COUNTRY
- [ ] CITY

The White House is in . . .

- [✓] THE USA
- [ ] MEXICO
- [ ] PAKISTAN

 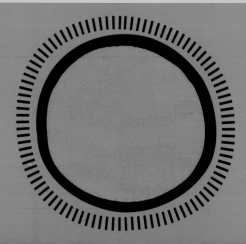

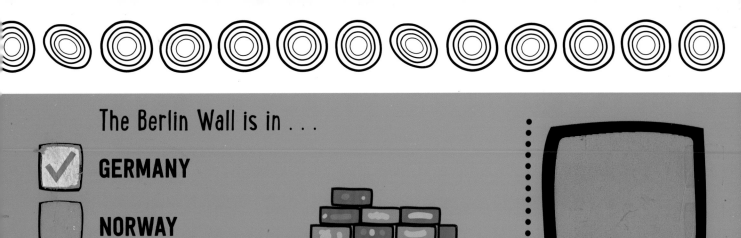

The Berlin Wall is in . . .

- ☑ **GERMANY**
- ☐ **NORWAY**
- ☐ **FINLAND**

Which one would Aztecs use for money?

- ☑ **COCOA BEANS**
- ☐ **AVOCADOS**
- ☐ **BANANAS**

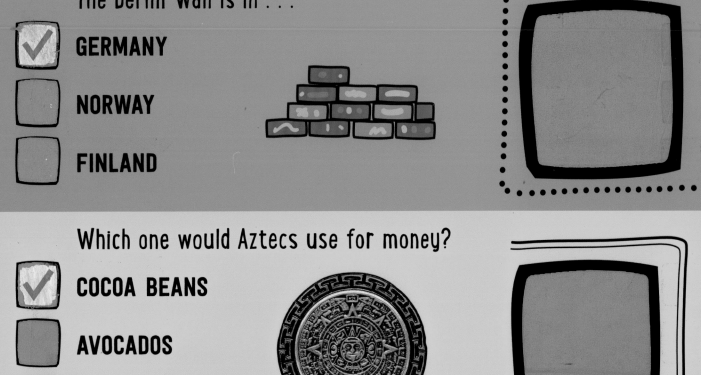

Which country used to use hieroglyphics?

- ☐ **MALAYSIA**
- ☐ **NEW ZEALAND**
- ☑ **EGYPT**

Where does it almost never snow?

- ☐ **THE NORTH POLE**
- ☑ **THE SAHARA DESERT**
- ☐ **THE ROCKY MOUNTAINS**

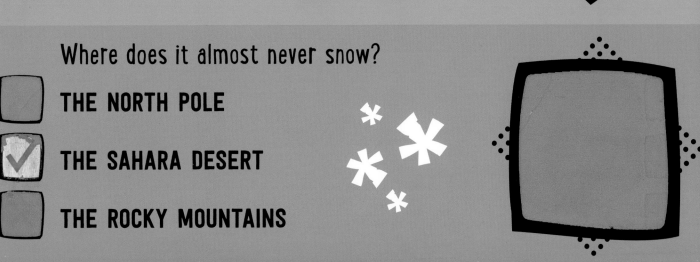

RIDDLE ME THIS!

Treasure is buried under one of the objects on the map. Solve the riddle, then scratch off the panel below the correct object to find the treasure!

I am very hard and round.
Don't confuse me with musical sounds.

N

TREASURE!

GUESS AGAIN

Solve these riddles about objects on the map.
Once you know the answer, scratch off the panel to see if you got it right!

Up, up, and up I go.
Stay back, for I might blow!

The more of me you take,
the more you leave behind.